C000002336

WORDS
AND
WHISPERS

WORDS AND WHISPERS

Passing thoughts and poems throughout the years

Miss Violeta Chalk

Copyright © 2022 Violeta chalk
Edited by Tayla Austin
ISBN: 979-8-8462-8667-2

All rights reserved. No part of this publication may be
Reproduced, distributed, or transmitted in any form by
Any means, including photocopying, recording, or other
Electronic methods, except in the case of brief quotations
Embodied in reviews and certain other non-commercial uses
Permitted by copyright law.

Thank you for supporting the authors rights.
First published august 2022

Dedication

This book is dedicated to the memory of my mother, who was an encouragement to me throughout my childhood.

To my sister, who believes in my ability to achieve my dream of having my poetry book published.

To the people I have known in my life; neighbours, friends, family, and my late husband. These poems wouldn't have been written if it wasn't for them inspiring me.

Contents

angels...1

crawley home sweet home..2

crawley town..3

crawley's blight 3

crawley thoroughfare...4

the memorial gardens 5

the long path 6

supermarkets in crawley...7

crawley's chimneys 8

to be...9

this road, st peters 10

the stagecoach 11

adison 12

tilgate park 13

thelma.. 14

so pleased 15

birthday.. 16

bills gardening tricks... 17

marriage 18

fighting back.. 19

a lovely soul 21

39 ¾ - never quite 40 22

remembering.. 23

dementia... 25

you've done it again adison 26

cissbury ring 27

findonite's reunion 28

lancing beach 29

a rose 30

gypsy dog 31

butterflies 33

the fair 34

landscape 35

trumpets 35

proud xmas tree 36

the garden views 37

bountiful 38

so much fun 39

wild 40

honoured 41

lunch in the garden 42

the view 43

sunflowers 44

our day 45

kaleidoscope 46

lady 47

the sound of life 48

i'm back in the garden 49

soldier of mine 50

Angels

Three puff like clouds,
One, two and three,
Disappearing over the tree.
There's many this shape,
Way up in the sky.
Like resting places for angels
That pass by.
The sky is so blue,
The angels can find a way through,
To people that need them
Like me, like you.

"My most recent poem, from July 2022."

Crawley home sweet home

Crawley is a great place to be,
It's got shops and the mall
Where you can have a spree.

It's got parks with slides and swings
And loads of exciting other things.
Basketball, climbing frames,
zip wire, a recent new game.

It's got the Hawth,
Where great shows are shown
And people who act there
Call it their own.

It's got clubs and pubs,
Food and drink,
And a good reputation,
I think.

So, here's to Crawley,
It's at the top.
The best spot in England,
It's got the lot.

Crawley town

Crawley was the town of old,
Struggling to be the new town untold.
I still like the old town,
I hope you do too.
Because of the old craftsmanship,
The new town pulled through.

Crawley's blight

The nurse's quarters are still there,
Empty darkroom and bare.
Pigeons fly all around, can't get in.
Boarded up sound,
This sticks out like a sore thumb.
The only blight on our town, well done.

Crawley thoroughfare

London to Brighton
The old crocs go,
Coming through Crawley
Oh, so slow.

The cars are great,
Giving an aura
Of a long-ago date.

They come to Crawley
on their special day,
Stop to rest
Then go on their way.

This adds something to Crawley,
Without a doubt.
I wish i got my camera out.

"My family and I used to watch these vehicles together in the high street most years."

The memorial gardens

The memorial garden is the place to be.
It's got hedges and plants and beautiful trees.
It's got lawns and benches
And parks, that twist and wind to different exits.

It's all quite fine,
People sit there any time of day
Sunning themselves while the children play.

One of its paths go to the mall,
Another to the town,
Another path has been found
Which ends at the playground.

Well, there's loads to do
And it doesn't cost a penny,
The parents are pleased too.

The long path

The long path is a wonder of nature.
It has flowers and trees,
Birds and bees,
Squirrels that play every day.

Magpie and crow,
Sparrows that roost low.
It has nest that are high
Where squirrels can see the sky.

Flowers of colours; yellow, mauve, and blue
And any other you can think of too.
Round neck rock doves fly around
Making a wingless sound.

Robin with his eyes so bright,
You can even see those eyes at night.
Pigeon cooing up above
For his mate, his love.

This path i walk everyday
Listening to church bells on my way.
Saint john's ringing loud and clear
Over Crawley, year after year.

Supermarkets in Crawley

Crawley supermarkets are spread over the town.
Asda has a car park, all around.
Sainsbury's in west green is now bigger than life
With people coming and going,

Husband and wife.
Tesco's at three bridges is handy too,
Loads of discounts to name a few.
Summer will bring Wilkinson

And almost everything in price will drop.
The new pound shop is full to the brim
With shoppers vying for everything.
So come to our town have a look around,
There is always something to be found.

Crawley's chimneys

The chimneys are tall,
The chimneys are small.
They are sometimes wide,
Just big enough to get a chimney sweep inside.
They are inglenook and Crawley's pride.
They belong to houses of old
Where stories were told,
Around the wood all aglow
Of 100 years ago, or so.
they tell of a different life
Of people who strived to work
On the land,
To put money in hand.
To keep Crawley on the map
Is something they didn't lack.
The chimneys with their smoke
And scent of burning wood,
Looked and smelled so good.
After work and play,
To welcome people home
At the break of day.
This legacy they have left
Is fascinating to see,
And just to think, it's been left there,
For you and for me.

"I still love these chimneys today."

To be

The wind you cannot see,
The sun you cannot touch.
The moon and stars visual,
Our planet immeasurable.

Time on the clock ticking away
From night-time into day.
Weeks also turned into months
And life plays its sweet song.

Of sun, wind, rain, and snow.
People busy to and fro.
Life goes on you see,
That's how it's meant to be.

This road, St Peters

I think back to a time
When this road was new.
Turn of the century, that will do.
A cold night of snow lanterns all aglow.

Chimneys with smoke billowing out.
That's what it was all about.
Imagine this road with no other houses.
Only fields and animals

And no roundabouts.
No one-way system to hamper your day,
Only horses and carts and bundles of hay.
What a great time that must have been.

Beautiful summers of golden green,
Meadows adorned with rare butterflies and plants.
Sun beaming down on the dance
Of the poppies in the wind there red all aglow.

A carpet of beauty,
How little do we know
Of that time when life was slow.

"St Peter's road is where my husband and I lived
together for 8 years and at different times all three sons
lived there too."

The stagecoach

Thundering through the countryside
With the coachman at their side.
The stagecoach with its horses four
Would stop at the George indoor.

People would alight
For food and wine and a pipe.
Horses well fed and rest
Would gallop on undo their best.

The stagecoach was the main way to travel
Over stone and gravel on the word they would go.
All those centuries, don't you know?

Adison

You wowed the crowd,
You stole the night.
With your slick performance,
You got it right.

We clapped and cheered
Until we were hoarse,
But you being Adison,
You stayed on course.

You proved to us
Without a doubt,
Winning is not
What it's all about.

So, here's to you Adison,
You're at the top.
A young man,
Who's got the lot.

"Adison is one of my 7th eldest grand-child and I'm so proud of his gift of dance."

Tilgate park

Walk along a path of trees
To a wood that stood for centuries.
Fallen logs, flowers, and frogs.
All these and more, right at our door.

The walked garden with its array of plants,
A rockery with flowers and grasses that dance.
In the sun rain also, there's a cafe where people dine
On cake and tea, after 9.

Children love the maze where they climb
And gaze across the way
On a hot summers day.

You can see pigs and goats, ducks that float
In the animal park before dark.
Red squirrels and cows,
Tortoises with hard shells.

Walk further along and you will see
Paths that wind endlessly.
The red root tree is smooth and clean,
It would make a fine beam.

Life in this park is easy and slow,
That's why people go
To Tilgate park, before dark.

Thelma

We stood side by side
Watching the great grandchildren
On the slide.
The chats we had were simple and true
Of your love of animals,
No doubt they will miss you.
We met, you and I
Through family ties.
Became great grandparents,
Until you died.
In heaven there's a place for you
Looking after the animals
That pass through.
so, I know you will be happy up above,
Looking after god's creatures
With his blessing, with his love.

So pleased

I'm so pleased you're up and about,
Planning to get the spade out.
In the garden growing things,
Sitting hearing birds sing.

Sun on face, in your own private space.
Cup of tea in your hand,
Eyes scanning the land.
Thinking of things to grow,

Cucumbers, tomatoes, all in a row.
Everything in your world, just right.
Happiness, contentment, from morning till night.

"This poem was written for my brother after he came out of hospital, and I wanted to cheer him up with a poem."

Birthday

Mum on your special day,
I wish you happiness in every way.
I hope the day starts with tea and toast
And later, a lunch along the coast.

Looking out across the sea
Thinking this is how it should be.
Birthdays come but once a year
But dining out shouldn't disappear.

So, pick a menu, every day.
Jump on a bus and go your way.
To a venue, wherever it may be.
Lunch, dinner, plus a coffee.

Bills gardening tricks

Bill is as busy as a bee,
Can't even stop for tea.
His spade is out he's digging about,
Hoping to finish the lawn in time.

So, he's measuring with a line.
He's a whiz with his spade,
Putting turf upside down laid.
The garden looks good, so it should.

He's out all day with his spade in hand
Altering the land.
Bill says Joan, that looks good I bet,
You're pleased you got that wood.

You've done us proud,
The garden looks great.
Now keep the dogs out
And shut that gate.

"This gentleman is my neighbour and i worte this poem for him 6 years ago."

Marriage

Marriage is a sacred thing.
You pick your day and then the bells ring.
Family come to wish you well,
As your husband lifts your veil.

People gather all around
For the picture, now don't frown.
Smile as if you're pleased to be
Standing next to your old auntie.

Love and warmth filled the air
As you sit on your chair.
Best man says his piece
just before the big feast.

Cake and champagne abound
Like confetti on the ground.
Everything is now said and done.
So put on the music and have some fun.

Auntie is up and about
Getting her knees out.
Back and forth, there she goes,
Where she lands nobody knows.

Having a great time is what it's all about
Hope she doesn't get anything else out.
Oh no, look in the bag she's got her cat.
Oh dear, she's sat on her hat.

Fighting back

[in more ways than one]

It's good you're fighting back,
Being positive is something you don't lack.
I'm glad you've got your bike.
What are you like?

Poodling along your way,
It gives you strength for another day.
Thrilled to bits with your bill's
Building tricks.

Making furniture out of wood,
Bill says it looks good.
Keeps out the wind and rain,
All it needs now is a windowpane.

Sit on board and ride about.
Bill tries to keep abreast
But with that speed,
He needs a rest.

Come on bill, you shout.
Keep up or we will run out.
The battery is on low,
How fast can you go?

I don't know, shouts bill
I'm stuck on this hill.
Keep going, says Joan,
We should make it home.

Right, says bill
Hold on tight, I bought a kite.
Here, if I stand on the rear,
Right back we should appear.

On a track over here,
What says Joan,
That's not home.
Where's your phone?
You got it wrong.

There's a train coming along,
Let's sing a song.
Why? Says bill.
It's all downhill,

We will soon be back,
Just need a push
On this track.

"Another poem for bill."

A lovely soul

A lovely soul has gone away
Leaving us bereft on this sad day.
Her memory is of beautiful things,
Colour and laughter,
Hearing her sing.
You touched us all
With your tenacity and strength,
Even when tears flowed and then were spent.
He never gave up, he never gave in.
Your love of life was the key
To the woman you were meant to be.

39 ¾ - never quite 40

The word is out, you are about
To have a birthday.
The lines are drawn,
Don't be forlorn.

It's laughter and tears
Down through the years
So, bring on the wine,
Bring on the song.

Dance, for the night is young.
You will be free
When fears flee.
To another year that you cannot see.

The life is grand, life is fun,
Just make time for everyone.
Leave the pots, leave the pans,
Take the children hand in hand.

To a place that you love best,
Put up your feet and have a rest.
Give up love to those around
And watch it come back in sure abound.

All that you're meant to be
Is in front of you
In sweet harmony.

Remembering

I'm missing you so much,
Now we're apart.
And it's an ache in my heart
That I left you there.

You were my little boy.
My sidekick.
My one and only true little friend,
Loyal to the end.

The days are long without you.
And memories flood in of younger years.
Of the laughter and tears,
Your naughty ways.

The hazy days of summer,
The romping in the park,
You running away,
And me finding you before dark.

So, so, lost without you my little boy.
But I'll always remember your handsome gaze,
And chasing anything in sight,
Even the man on his motorbike.

Me and you walking in the woods
Was your favourite thing.
Me hiding behind the trees,
Hearing birds sing.

You looking for me
Left and right,
Excited wag of the tail
When you had me in sight.

Beautiful boy it so sad,
My years start to fall,
If time could not stand still,
Then I wouldn't be crying at all.

I never thought
A little dog like you,
Would have this affect,
But you do.

so lost without you,
If only I could touch you again.
And sit with you, gazing at the stars,
Like we used to do on a quiet evening, just us two.

*"To Charlie, so blessed and happy that we had you in our lives
for fifteen years. Love you always and forever. Your human
sidekick".*

Dementia

Dementia is here to stay.
It doesn't pick rich or poor,
It knocks on any door.
It stops the brain and leave the body in pain.
It drains the soul of life apart
And it has no heart.
Dementia is mainly for the old
So we're told, but if that's true;
What are we going to do?
Because young is old, so the future is told.
The young will help, I have no doubt.
Direct them in the right way and they will say
Don't wait until tomorrow, sort it today.
You're okay.
They don't want our legacy of un-care,
Head in the sand,
So please get the problem in hand.

You've done it again Adison

You've done it again Adison,
You've won the night.
You're back on form
And you got it right.

Good luck for the future,
Whatever it may bring.
If you win again,
Give us a ring.

We are pleased to bits
With your dancing tricks.

Cissbury ring

Up lane, over downs,
Cissbury ring was the place to go.
In winter in the snow,
We would walk across a world of white.
From morning till night,
This is where romans trod
So long ago.
We ascend the fortress
Looking over land, what a lot.
The romans left artefacts
Of coins and tools and all that.
Treasure was dug and found
Somewhere underground.

Findonite's reunion

Findon reunion was great.
We all met there on the appropriate date.
The villager was the name of the venue.
We all met there after two.

We gathered round and sometimes frowned
At the people across the room.
They looked back with a smile
And in a while, they frowned too.

My name is sim, my name is long,
And so, this chatter carried on.
until all names were said and done.

Then we talked about this and that,
Then got up from where we sat.
Met people from the past
Who were in our class.

People there came from far and wide
It was nice standing there, side by side.
Working out who was who, was very hard to do
But soon we cottoned on, to who was who.

Eventually we all settled down,
Had our lunch without a frown.
We all said we would meet up soon,
Perhaps someone in June?

Lancing beach

At last, we are there
At the beach and don't have a care.
Sun beating down on the hot sand,
Little stones and pebbles all around.

The water clear and blue,
Course on, oh so new.
Running down the sand in my worn-out shoes.
Stopping at the water's edge to look at the view.

There are small boats bobbing up and down
And people fishing all around.
Kites flying way up high
And children laughing running by.

Bucket and spade in hand,
Mum helps digging in the sand.
I walk farther into the salty sea
And start swimming and so happy to be.
Here on this beach of my dreams
Where lots of people go, it seems.

"A beach I wish I had the time to visit more often."

A rose

A rose of beauty
A flower of love
Followed by a white turtledove
This rose I give to you
Making a wish
That will come true.

"My first poem in 1995"

Gypsy dog

They said you are a gypsy dog,
They said you ran away.
They said you had a chain around your neck
When they had found you that day.

They told me you had bit someone
And your life was about to end.
I could not bear it, so I made you
My best friend.

I took you in my arms
To carry you away
But you had other thoughts
And bit me on that day.

I was going to leave you
And went to turn away
But then I saw a tender heart
Amongst the disarray.

Benji, I named you.
Forever in my heart.
A rogue dog that fought me
From the very start.

Never have I known a dog
So faithful and so true,
Who saved my life,
Just like I saved you.

So lost without you,
My naughty little gypsy dog.
You made me laugh and cry.
I will never forget you,
until the day I die.

"Benji came into my son's life at the age of ten and we love the little rogue like he was family."

Butterflies

So many colours, so beautiful.
Delicate, entrancing
Fluttering here and there.
In a sunlit wood
Playing with their mates.
Dancing, spiralling,
In mid-air.
Their wings so perfectly formed,
Flying free, without a care.

"A poem that I wrote a mother who needed it."

The fair

The sheep fair is here at last,
Coconut shies, fish to be won.
Bumper cars, oh, so much fun.
Swing boats that go way up high,
You both pull a rope and touch the sky.
Rifle range, a pound a shot,
Prizes to be won, oh what a lot.
Caravans, long, made of wood,
Painted in bright colours,
Looks so good.
The fair is here, every year,
Gathering crowds from every sphere.
looking for bargains galore,
Spending their money, that's for sure.
Chickens and ducks for sale,
Sheep grazing on the bails.
Sun shining down, what a glorious day.
People happy in every way.

Landscape

Rabbit and pheasant, butterfly, and bee.
Flowers of all colours that we can see.
Horse in the distance and hills behind
Making a landscape that wouldn't be hard to find.
Hollyhocks, cornflower, poppy, and tree.
A cat looking on eagerly.
A beautiful picture
With every colour to be found.
Completes the look, all around.

Trumpets

The colours are many.
Pale blue and yellow, red and mauve,
Red and white, pink and white, just pink.
Making a spectacle of their glorious state,
Hanging from baskets by garden gate.
Everywhere outside pubs
In city centres along the highways and byways.
So plentiful in their glowing glory
A cascade of colour, like no other.

Proud xmas tree

Christmas tree so tall,
Grown from a baby so small.
Your bows count the years
Of the owner you have cheered.
In your quest for height
You stand 20 feet tall.
Too big to bring in a house too small.

"My husband planted this tree in 2004 and we brought it with us to our last home together."

The garden views

The clouds move across the sky
Altering as they go,
Making different shapes
Like a crocodile, and a woodman in the snow.

Funny looking duck with a curled-up tail,
A one-eyed monster on the prowl.
Birds still flying about across their path,
Not knowing what is there

But birds being birds don't have a care.
From my view of sky and land
There is lots to see,
Like aerials on chimneys so you can watch tv.

White butterflies are gently gliding about
While vegetables are ready to sprout.
Flowers in their multitude of colours
Make my day so beautiful in their array.

A raised flower bed so lush with blooms,
Bees and creatures that fly
All fluttering down from the sky.
Collecting nectar, at every flower, hour after hour.

Our little fountain imitating a bubbling brook,
The sound audible, the price affordable.
Seagulls calling me to sea -
If only I had a boat, I would go there with glee.

Bountiful

Standing proud like soldiers on parade,
The white daisy, yellow centre.
Crowded together in unison
Green foliage abounds.
With leaves outnumbering
The many buds and flowers
Of this truly beautiful
Creation of nature.

So much fun

Being a child was so much fun,
Trees to climb, places to hide
Fields to run.
Bows and arrows were made and played,
Helping the milk men on a sunny day.
Delivering milk was child's play
Being pulled across the snow on a sledge
Was quite fine.
I'm playing skipping, with mums washing line.
Climbing trees was boy's work
But us girls didn't shirk.
Up we would shimmy,
Without a care
The boys were impressed, glad we were there.

Wild

Gliding on the wind so high,
Seagulls' overhead way up in the sky.
Swooping and calling their flock together,
Crying in the wind.

They're big and strong
With wings quite long.
Eyes that scan the horizon
For food for their tea.

They can be quite troublesome you see,

And downright amazing.

Honoured

A sensitive soul flying around,
Disguised as a butterfly
Landing on the ground,
Its wings gossamer, made of fine silk.

Colours so delicate, powder blue and white,
Peacock colours so rich all the way through.
Yellow butterfly, now rarely seen.
If I could see one, I would feel like the queen.

For nature is under diminished,
In these virus-like times.
Not to see a rare butterfly,
Is simply divine.

I sit in my garden studying the view
Hoping a rare butterfly will glide its way through.
And when one does, I'm happy as can be
And the thought of its beauty will stay with me.

So, when you're in your garden
And the butterfly you see,
You are very honoured
For all of eternity.

"One of my best poems."

Lunch in the garden

A little dog with bent over ears,
Floats across the sky, then disappears.
A man with a bull on his lap
And hair that's not all that.
Floating away joining up with clouds, big and small,
Till it's one and covers all.
Tiny bits of a cloud, make a figure running.
Another one doing acrobats, the performance is quite stunning
A head and face appear with dog ears
and a large nose, hopefully he can hold that pose.
Now another cloud has joined his face,
Now it looks like a race
To see what shapes the cloud can make.
Now it's a big stag beetle, eating some cake.

The view

The view is green of leaf,
White of flower.
Sparrows flying through the maze of leaves every hour
Of the day, until dusk breaths its heavy sigh
And night-time draws its cloak around the day.
Day cosies down for a well-earned rest
Until the sun opens the best of the day.
The myriad kaleidoscope of colour
Reflected by the sun.
Spreading over land
Until the day is done.

Sunflowers

Sunflowers yellow and brown,
Growing tall out of the ground.
Bees gathered on the brow
Collecting nectar is their thing.
Taking it home on the wing.

Our day

Our day starts at eight,
With the postman opening our gate.
Letters fall through the door,
Pick them up, anymore?

Then go to make tea,
Have some toast
And being Sunday
Put on a roast.

Prepare the veg,
Carrots and peas,
Broccoli, potatoes
And some more of these.

Kaleidoscope

Trees of green, against the blue sky,
Big cotton like balls passing by.
Waiting for the picture to change,
Into animals, all things we cannot see.
For clouds of wondrous creativity,
Without painting a single thing.
Clouds change into what we want them to be,
But where I sit there are no clouds,
so, I'll move to where they are allowed.

Lady

Little dog
So trim and quick,
You made us laugh
With every little trick.

You've been a light,
In our lives, forever and a day.
Sweet little girl,
Always ready for play.

We will miss you so much,
Our lives won't be the same.
We will forever be grateful,
That you came our way.

"My neighbour Celia's dog."

The sound of life

The sound of pigeons,
Flapping in the tree,
Eating berries for their tea.

Flies buzzing overhead,
Seagulls cooling time for bed.
Motorbikes roaring away,
People motoring home, from that day.

I'm back in the garden

In my garden it's different this year,
I've left the plants to grow
Without pulling out the row
Of weeds or grass, they've been left to sow.

So, the garden can die off
And slowly disappear,
It could take all year.
Fed up with weeding and the like,
It can all take a hike.

I'm not moaning you see,
It's just a phase.
The older I get,
The more I laze.

Backbreaking work
Is no longer for me.
I'd rather have a Victoria sponge
And a nice cup of tea.

Soldier of mine

Soldier of mine, you came through,
To be with your family,
Is something you had to do.
At home was the best care you had,
Looked after, my husband, their dad.
Your life was not in vain
As you had much family who loved you
And felt the same.
Caring for you
Was the right thing to do,
As for three months
Loneliness was all you knew.
So, here's to my soldier first
And then the man,
Who showed us all that pain-longing,
Can get you home
To be with the family,
No longer alone.

"Dedicated to my husband David"

Thank you.

Printed in Great Britain
by Amazon

85136960R00034